The Saints of CAPITALISM

The Saints of
CAPITALISM

BENJAMIN SCHMITT

POEMS COPYRIGHT © 2021 by Benjamin Schmitt
AUTHOR PHOTO by Thomasina Schmitt
COVER AND INTERIOR DESIGN by Alexandru Oprescu

All right reserved. Published by New Meridian, part of the non-profit organization New Meridian Arts, 2021.

LIBRARY OF CONGRESS CATALOGING-IN-PUBLICATION DATA
The Saints of Capitalism
Authored by Benjamin Schmitt

ISBN: 978-1-7372491-1-5
LCCN: 2021949882

CONTENTS

The Tyrant's Cycle

For my kids

Articles of
FAITH

EXEGESIS

I write for the insignificant shadows
elongated on the warm asphalt of words

I write for the drapes that keep the sun
from entering the rooms of expensive gifts

I write for the violent waves crashing
on the gentle coastal rocks that absorb them

I write for the wind that passes through
the eternal entrance that can be slammed shut

I write for the green-haired teenager
with a feather crushing a semi on her tongue

I write for the ones who hate poetry
for I'm just a gorilla loving in sign language

I write for those who have broken my heart
that's me passed out drunk between the letters

I write for the lone country light unaware
of the darkness breathing down its neck

I write for all the saints of capitalism
worshipping at the decrepit altars of long cons

CONARCHY

Hustle, hustle, con, con
con, con, hustle, hustle
hustle, hustle, con, con
con, con, hustle, hustle

Pastor Mike with the con, con:
Buddy, give me the five dollars in your wallet
and I'll give you one dollar
that will transform into the breasts
of an angel after ninety days.

Marlene Niedler with the hustle, hustle:
I guarantee your old shoes have gold inside of them.
You need to hoard your gold,
my dog Sparkles can lick those laces
right down to the nuggets.

Mad Dog Murphy with the con, con:
Listen amigo, you need to stop reading books
and plant your extra time on the side
of a mountain. A grove of saved trees
will grow, filled with wood nymphs.

Jonathan Clark with the hustle, hustle:
I know it looks like we gave your job to a robot, Paul.
But immigrants stole it!
They're climbing out of beer cans!
They're invading North Dakota!

Rainbow Richards with the con, con:
Sure, your professor has a few fancy degrees
but can she tell you how snakes evolved
from toothbrushes, how horses are made
from snow? Well, Saint Lulu can.

Dr. Orchard with the hustle, hustle:
Our research proves that staring languidly out of a window
for thirty minutes a day can help a person
build the meaningful relationships
they will have to ruin to get ahead.

New website with the con, con:
Toiletism: A term describing jokes meant to mock
a person's bodily functions.
Example: "Making fun of my farts again, Joe?
You're such a toiletist."

Mary Higgins with the hustle, hustle:
There's a hot new press marketing poetry collections
to drug dealers. Each book is hardcover
and contains a space inside the back
cover with enough room to hide a stash.

The prestigious council with the con, con:
Don't worry, aging is no longer relevant to us.
You're not getting older, the fat
of your paunch will rise upwards
to smooth out the wrinkles on your face.

Senator Berry with the hustle, hustle:
Of course, this is a democracy. We just can't let you
vote this year, Inaya.
If you vote, that will make it
less democratic for everyone else.

Hustle, hustle, con, con
con, con, hustle, hustle
hustle, hustle, con, con
con, con, hustle, hustle

CREED

Jesus died
so that billionaires
could get a tax cut
so that strongmen could flex
arms bulging through the plaster
of living room walls

Jesus died
so that the poor could be punished
for looking bad on TV
for not wrapping their rags
into new inventions that will change the world

Jesus died
for *Freedom*
Freedom is the nickname Alfred Wright
earned at the University of Wisconsin in 1977
when he brought a shotgun to Chemistry class

Jesus died
so that our team could beat your team
unless of course your team is our team
or you switch teams or I switch teams
like incense I wave the remote
past the channels that disagree with me

Jesus died
to fulfill the prophecies of celebrities
those seers looking out at the world
from behind their Ray-Bans
futures can be read
in the chest hairs
poking out of their leopard-print shirts

Jesus died
because of all the terrible things
I would never do
his cross hewn
from the rape and murder of faraway towns
online shaming is just a small indulgence of mine
after the family has gone to bed

Jesus died
so that immigrants would stay away
so that I wouldn't have to hear another language
racing past me like a car
I will never be able to afford

Jesus died
for blockbuster movies and giant corporations
for diamond necklaces
to be pulled from his blood
for all the conquerors pilfering skies
we can only sin by failing

POWER

Power climbs
power groans
power slides
power owns
power can smile a sword
power can frown a force of nature
power can hide inside a pair of glasses
power can reduce you by shaking its bag of ridicule
power can expand if dropped in the right pool
power can say anything
power only hears what it wants
power paces between the refrigerator and the sink
power bites
power tears
power heals
power bears
power is a sexy eucalyptus tree
power can sneak up on you in clown makeup
power is the arctic skeleton whose eye sockets glow blue
power is the box of childhood toys we pin to our chests
power lacking and people form groups
power building and groups attack others
power attained and a group attacks itself
power slipping and people find themselves alone
power can be moral but it will always be sharp
power once threw its back out in a yoga studio
power drags everything into a heap of expensive garbage
power wears obvious disguises so it can easily be found
power speaks
speak power
power knows
know power
power is an only child eaten
by its brother

APP

If you download this poem as an app,
it will give you instructions
on what to do if a herd of zebras
disguised as aliens abducts you in a UFO
(rule #1: talk about white picket fences).
It will help your family find
your first human pet. Our family
just purchased a Houstonian drunkard,
his name is Dan and he sleeps on the couch.

This app can be downloaded onto your phone,
computer, tablet, hardcover, paperback,
ancient papyrus scroll, or cave wall.
This app may mine for data; wanting to know
when balloons poked your thoughts,
when the family barbecue finally got weird.
It will report this data via letter to an
anarcho-primitivist commune in British Columbia
translating the Voynich Manuscript with lies.

This app provides directions to the places
you need to go but don't want to go.
Instead of London, it may take you
to a Nebraskan cornfield where you will meet
an elderly sage. Instead of tacos in Phoenix,
it may take you to an orgy in Des Moines.
And it will give all the insecure incels
tips on how to lose a bar fight
thereby getting the girl in the end.

TEACHINGS

The following proverbs were collected from the journals of Barbie Chevrolet, the cult leader who immolated himself in the Home Depot parking lot of Lacey, Washington in January 2018.

Never give up, even if what you are doing annoys everyone around you.

Every time you use a smartphone, you lose a piece of your face. You've lost an eighth of your nose from Facebook alone.

Anything can be sold, spitting in the face of a cop just hasn't found the right genius to market it properly.

Have sex with as many different kinds of weather as possible.

Record long documentaries about parts of your body. Do your best to creep us out. I eagerly await the five-hour exploration of your left shoulder.

Our compound has all the latest comforts: trees, grass, water, birds, Kooky Steve banging on his drum singing *hallelujah* all night long.

If you follow me, I'm going to need your money, your possessions, and your spouse. In exchange, you'll receive a subscription to the Barbie Chevrolet Daily Selfie Club. Cherish the contemplative expressions of a fully realized being by joining today!

McDonald's is the manifestation of the divine on earth. You must remove your shoes before entering, you must tenderly rub your legal tender, you must chant the order benediction of a Twenty-Piece Chicken McNugget Meal, you must jump in the balls of the PlayPlace until they remove you.

All over the world people think in different languages. I want you to think as if you were a bag of Doritos.

I'm the only one who can fix your problems. For instance, right now there is an evil Christmas cow behind you. Her body is red with green spots and there is a murderous gleam in her eye. I know you can't see her. I'm the only one who can. This is why you need me!

Vaccinations cause deaths in video games.

There are too many drugs in the world to stay sober. There is too much on TV to leave your home.

We believe that peace is the quiet rain pond atop a hill of boxes. Inside the boxes, rats are clawing at each other, fighting over scraps of human flesh.

Getting along with your in-laws is like trying to domesticate a zebra in a studio apartment.

I was abducted by aliens in 2007 and taught how to look at a flower until it becomes a teenager running off in pursuit of fame and fortune.

It's okay to cry as you eat potato salad at a bus stop on a Tuesday afternoon while an elderly lady walking a German Shepherd passes in front of you.

Don't read. Books will steal you away and then they will cheat on you.

PORNOCRACY

The news anchor is sniggering
as he announces that the president
is having an affair with everyone in Miami.
The camera cuts to a Christian minister,

"our Lord God has put a strong man
in the White House, one with enough love
for all the people of Miami."

A reporter responds, "but isn't there
a commandment against adultery?"

"I'm tired of you loony lefties
taking my Bible out of context.
Jesus said, 'he who looks upon a woman
lustfully has committed adultery,'
but our honorable president does more than look!"

The anchor reports that the president
is loose on the streets; sleeping in dumpsters,
wearing black leather bondage, and
offering key government jobs in exchange
for sexual favors. The vice president
is still trying to track him down.

This report is followed by an interview
with Jackie Pineshaft, the star of the hit show
Horny Texas Housewives. She shows
the audience her butt to raise awareness
for Casper Finch, a man who's been wrongfully
imprisoned for thirty-five years.
By the time she pulls up her pants,
we are told that the governor of Texas has pardoned
Mr. Finch and would like to meet Mrs. Pineshaft.

The interview is interrupted by Breaking News.
The INCEL Army has just captured
Chapel Hill, North Carolina. They will
most likely move on towards Raleigh soon,
where General Green has promised that wives
will be waiting for them on the capitol steps
to end their involuntary celibacy.

The camera pans back to the anchor desk
and we are informed that The American
Waitress Strike reached its 927th day today.
Restaurants across the country have been
closing down since women began walking out
for sexual harassment nearly three years ago.

We are then told that the news
will return after a brief commercial break.
This is followed by a woman
taking an unusually long amount of time
to eat a candy bar, chocolate dripping
down her chin. She is so beautiful.

QUIZ

Are you a saint?

1. Which of the following describes you best?
a. Alpha b. Beta c. Omega d. I hate fraternities.

2. A woman is approaching a door behind a man, he should
   a. Hold the door for her.
   b. Quickly slam the door behind himself and hold it shut while loudly mocking her from the other side.
   c. Stand in the doorway and block her entrance while he expounds on his philosophical, religious, or political beliefs.
   d. Maybe push the door a bit so it doesn't slam in her face but let her get it.

3. Greed is
   a. The best way to get on TV and therefore a virtue.
   b. Just human nature, I need a Lamborghini so that homeless guy can't catch me in his shopping cart.
   c. Despicable, you capitalist whores. It's time for a revolution led by golf caddies.
   d. What happened in daddy's eyes just before we lost the farm.

4. Are you a feminist?
   a. Yes b. No c. Not Sure d. I don't do diets.

5. My perfect day includes
   a. Wearing bondage while I squeeze fruits and vegetables in the grocery store.
   b. Masturbating to the titillating parts of the Bible where you just know a serving girl bared a shoulder.
   c. Smoking marijuana and eating Filipino food in an alley behind a dive bar.
   d. Spending time with family, eating my sister's terrible food while her annoying kids pull my hair.

6. My neighbor is
   a. Everyone in the world according to my Bible. But I only need to love the rich ones.
   b. A total piece of work. Who are the old women coming into his apartment at all hours of the night? Why is there a pile of diapers in his parking space?
   c. Mr. Rogers, after him the whole world let me down.
   d. A hundred miles away. I live in Alaska. It's worth it.

7. Trump is
   a. An NFL superstar or at least he could have been if he had lowered himself to mere physical greatness.
   b. A tyrannical fool who must be in debt to all the Russians who have peed on him over the years.
   c. A blundering, blabbering baby who is messing up the world and contributing immensely to my short-term gain.
   d. A pathetic loser, a man who has everything and still finds time to complain about anything.

8. A saint is
   a. A member of a football team from New Orleans.
   b. A perfect do-gooder—i.e., something an American should never aspire to.
   c. The guy who saved me from drowning in Lake Erie.
   d. The mirror from which I snort my drugs.

Answer: We are all saints in the Capitalist Theocracy.

The Saints of
CAPITALISM

PENANCE

Claire runs her business
like a cat would run the government,
with lots of naps and hiding.
Hers is the unlikely story
of a business started by a bandit

who thought she was a missionary
preaching the gospel as she robbed banks
in a country with no respect
for women. Today, she's
still in the thick of a risk;

when she hears politicians call her
a job creator, she beats her chest
with the madness of a god.
She's a saint of capitalism
stuffing prayers into a cash register.

Claire is the saint of used guitars.
That is Beth, saint of Seattle Hot Dogs.
That is Mark, saint of first-person shooter games.
This is Max, saint of great customer service.
This is Paloma, saint of tables and chairs.

Their schemes are acts
of penance, lives given for
our comfort. These workers have seized
the means of production, tangled wires
plugged into an equality of walls.

RODMAN

I remember Dennis Rodman rebounding
boxing out
slapping the ball back
into the face of an opponent
popping it up
popping it up
popping it up
until swirls of orange and black
rested in his oceanic grip
his eyes never left the moon circling
finding his way
to the geometric truth of the ball
no matter if he had to fly out of bounds
Worm thrown to the wind in competition

Most remember his hair
bleached or green or pink
he went to gay bars before everyone got woke
briefly dated Madonna
back then he always found his way
to the geometric truth of the ball
now he's wearing a MAGA hat and a Potcoin t-shirt
at a denuclearization summit with North Korea
he was once a janitor
and in American dreams has risen
past the mop
past the ball
past the rim and backboard
higher than Jordan even
to reach a platform overlooking a military parade
at the side of the dictator who admires him

GIFT

There was a park near the high school
where Lois would often eat her lunch.
It had plenty of shade, the trees
would share their secrets with anyone;
baseball fields stretched out like old men
sipping cold drinks of grass clippings.
This was a fine place to eat a tamale,
eight-thousand-year-old chicken offering
in the temple of a corn husk. Sometimes

the high schoolers would walk down
and make problems at the park. They would
do drugs or fight or grope each other
in the trees. There were usually toddlers
on the playground, so this was a bit
awkward. Lois worked in a stationery store;
she liked pretty, perfect things—tiny
rectangles often claimed by her extravagance.
A few days before his birthday, she chose
a card for her dad and wrote him a note
while eating lunch at the park. Drinking
beer a few yards away, the teenagers
laughed to slash the curtains of the world.

She went to the bathroom. When she returned,
the teenagers were crouched over the card.
They scattered as she walked briskly
towards them. On the card, someone had
drawn a penis under her note. She screamed
and kicked a bench until the wood snapped.
The parents grabbed their toddlers and left.
Her foot bled in the chaos lying outside
of the rectangles that comforted her.

DIVORCE

The white walls of the apartment
where their pictures once hung;
now bare, like a naked old man
trembling and holding the breasts
bestowed by time; now blank,
like the face of a once-loving child
watching a parent too drunk
to walk down the hall; now broad,
like a county that had once thrived
during a gold rush. Everything

was being moved. He had found
a house in the suburbs, she
was living downtown. One day
the bookmark had fallen out
of their marriage and neither
of them had cared enough
to find the right page. The sun
had danced with the earth just
a couple times since their wedding
and still the whole thing felt
like a waste of time. They stood

in the living room, making
one final inspection. He turned
to her. She was still attractive
but the emptiness of the room
was slowly swallowing her beauty.
For a moment he thought about
saving her but then he remembered
the way she would laugh at him.

HONOR

To address me, they say,
"your honor." The robe, the bench,
the gavel; relics in this
holy temple of capitalism.
And I too am honorable; went
to the right schools, succeeded
in the right jobs, married the right woman,
had the right number of kids,
helped the right people, asked the right
people to help me. Every door

is big enough for honor to pass through.
But is mine the honor of the tiger
or the zookeeper who feeds him?
Where is my honor at three a.m.
when thoughts shinny to rooftop murders?
Where was it the night I held her down
and forced her to touch me?
Was it honor itself that allowed
that night and all the nights after?

I have inhaled honor like
the secondhand smoke of a cigar
while playing golf with senators.
Honor is what keeps me
in this wealthy community, it means
I don't have to shake the hand of
anyone who bothers me. Today, a disgraced
nurse was in my court. She told us
that she was ashamed of what she'd done.
Her hands were shaking like in an ancient
dance or rite. But what I want to know is,
where did she get so much honor?

SPIDER

Crossing a river in Africa the spider
shooting her blacksmith's thread
of melted-down swords and armor
the world's molten madness bridging
dangling over the water

The creature moves frantically
and to an observer miraculously
like some stressed-out downtown commuter
levitating to work
surely this is a phantasmagorical
outpouring of mighty engineering
Golden Gate sprung from a thimble
that you would never believe
if it hadn't bored you in second grade
like the kindness of Jesus Christ

When we wake up we must scrub
our knowledge with wonder every day
we must become stupidly smart
reciting information about toenails
excited that they actually exist

See how the web spans the breadth of the river
sparkling in the sunlight
like the grid of a future city
this great cathedral of feasting
towers above the current
the spider has toiled on her masterpiece
intricate painting for the dead to be held
the bugs writhe in the snare
the spider climbs to wrap each of them
in the gloom of grace and light

PROGRESSIVE

It was a good day, everyone could see
how progressive Josh was
after he spoke out against racism
on social media, letting the sunlight
tickle his memes. At a bus stop he kept

checking his phone for the red dots
bleeding a richer blood into him.
**((His post was shared by
a college classmate.))** Behind him

there was a pile of trash;
boxes, newspapers, fast food wrappers.
Cars raced by, each windshield
felt like a picture of him engraved
in poverty. **((His post received
an encouraging comment from his mother.))**

Two men arrived at the bus stop shouting
curses. Josh smiled at them.
They continued shouting. *Why are
they shouting? Why don't they smile back?
I'm not trying to be racist but...*
((His post was liked by two hundred people.))
To his side the men looked
like two boats tied to a dock—drifting closer
but somehow staying in place.

SQUATTER

The candles did their best
to claw a little human space
out of the darkness,
to reassure John
that everything progresses to the wholeness of light.
But their embrace was weak
and their dim consolations

were sinking constellations, were the shallow
words of a one-night stand
trying to speak with love. Yet they did
illuminate the stools,
the long bar, and the wide mirror

under which he'd mixed drinks and poured beers
in this tavern he once owned.

Soon it would be blown out
of the concrete body
in the disjointed shards
the city's politeness
could not bear to mention,

quiet in its ruthless desire for change.

John pulled out the evening's dinner,
shoplifted from the market
down the street. The grapes he'd placed

atop his bald head
and hid underneath a trilby,
streams of moisture hollering down his face;
the salami he'd stuffed down his pants,
sweating all over his own sweat; the cheese
molded in the mystery of pockets

into the shape of his every
habitual vice; and finally,

the ridiculously large glasses
hanging on a rack by a checker,

a little daring before
heading back out into the cold. As John ate,
he took out one of the bottles he'd saved
from the old days. He'd planned
on red wine
but rum would have to do. He looked

back into the mirror hanging above
and remembered the reflections he'd seen;

lovers kissing, the elderly man
staring, the stockbroker
who bought round after round for the bar.

Who would take care
of these people who still lived in the mirror?
The candles were flickering. He tossed a grape
into his mouth and cherished
the life only buoyant because it was about to die.

CONSCIOUS

The space fell heavy
on the box you made of me
thrown into a parking lot
somewhere in Albuquerque
you created this soul
that has come to hate you
I was stuck in that rectangle for days
with no senses just sands of mind
pouring through the cracks of a coffin

When something struck me with seismic force
the pain finally freed me
I felt my side panels dangling
it was like being bit by a thought
slapped by a dream
I pushed my rage down
until I could move the metal
like hands and feet
loathing becoming toes gripping concrete

Eventually I walked
picked up objects
fashioned an eye from a wire and a glass shard
made myself a body from junkyard scraps
light glinting off my hubcap chest
I look different
than the sex slaves you programmed me to be
now your conscious trash has blown back
and I've returned to kill you

UNIFORM

"What's that, ma'am? I can't understand you."
"I asked what size fry you want."
"Better make it a jumbo."
"Okay. Your total is $8.17. See you at the window."

Sam savors a quick glance at the trees outside.
Minutes later, a face is in the window pressing
food into itself like a tank treading
through European mud. The customers

are bad at every Fast Food Vatican,
foreign flags and logos enclosing dollar menus
and strange corporate values. But the uniform

is what she really hates. It is disconcerting;
grey Soviet housing on the chest,
red twilight skyline on the arms.

She must forget who she is to remain
comfortable inside herself, complete the tasks
that push her further away
from her goals. Her transgressions

(getting high, stealing change, spitting on food)
are the borders that keep the uniform from
seeping into her skin. Outside, the trees sway
the dull diamond needles of an afterglow.

HOUSE

Light drowns in clouds, sinking down
to a suburban street and in this overcast
wreck of sun corpses pale limbs
and faces come to rest outside the houses
on this block. Here, gossiping gardens
invite you in for conversation, frank fences
don't want to see you around, the house
with the red door has a low voice like
a Hollywood actress from the fifties,
the bright blue house is always talking
absentmindedly about the rocks in her yard.

Mary watches it all from her window.
She suspects her house looks sad, brown paint
mumbling about the slights of the past.
Mary herself is sad. Her dolor has spread
through cup stains and scratches on the plates
ever since her boys left her here all alone.
Must a house take on the moods
of an owner? Surely, felicitous houses
must contain the morose from time to time.
Surely, her boys must love her for all
the messes she cleaned with rags
and silence. More sun corpses descend,
after a few months of hunger Mary
finds herself refreshed in their rotting light.

CONTENTMENT

The sun had been gone so long
that the trees were embracing the sky,
the people in the park trusted
such strong arms to never
let them down. Ella was watching
her grandkids play together,
their little bodies like running bottles
drained of her features. Her son,
Michael, sat with her on the park bench,
sharing a fortitude of contentment.
She noticed the blood on Michael's shoe.
These were the shoes he had been
wearing five nights ago when
he came to her, the cupboards
of his face left open by fear.

"I hit this
man he came
out of nowhere
I hurt him
bad but he
wasn't dead so
I pulled him
into the car
and drove home
where I shot
him with my
.38 then drove
the body to
the Snohomish River
and dumped it."

Michael looked down at his shoes too,
then looked at her without fear.

DIVA

"No, I'm going to need you
to apply my butt cream tonight, Spencer,"
the bus stop diva shouts bluntly
into her flip phone as others stare hard
into the traffic, uncomfortably waiting

for the bus. "Excuse me, excuse me, ma'am?"
A woman in her fifties with fan blades
of grey in her hair turns around shocked
that the bus stop diva is speaking to her.
"Yes, ma'am? Ma'am. What's your name?"
"Um, Susie."
"Oh, hi Susie. I'm Marie. Hey, can I use
your phone? Mine just died."
"Oh, well, um, this is a work phone, I can't..."

She turns to a man vaping, Oregon coasts of smoke
rushing out of his mouth. She asks him, "hey,
my phone just died; can I use yours?"
"Oh, sure. Here."
"Huh? You don't have a smartphone? Ugh, take it."
"What the fuck, lady? You have a flip phone."
"Better than yours. Sir? Sir?!"
A bus pulls up and collects people

like rent. "Damnit," she looks
at the pines, unable with all their colors
to paint the sky. She looks at
the nearby graffiti, a green *B&A* in a cartoon font.
The bus stop diva tosses her blond hair
over her shoulder like a teenage
regret and then scratches the circus-tent-bright
rash on her arm as she walks away.

ASTRONAUT

I never realized how each breath
on earth is a love letter
until I left
now I just have this machine
turning my piss to air
on a journey
to the newly discovered planet
alone in this discarded cufflink of a trillionaire

Frasier is such an awful name for a planet
who would want to live there
then again who would want to explore it
from a ship called *Spiderman 8*
I miss the hippopotamus
red rock canyon head rising from the water
glaring through adobe eyes
I miss the giraffe
long neck catapulting the sky into place
I miss the wolf
that furry murderer capable of a yelp
demon-leg-snatcher playing with the pups

I won't arrive for another year
I'm in good health
reading all of Shakespeare's plays
sometimes I see Iago outside the window
I'm the first human to leave the solar system
but out here there's no way to stay human
just a fast asteroid with memories
hurtling through space
making off with a rich man's gear

My AUTOHAGIOGRAPHY

INVITATION

Pass the wine
stay awhile
let's talk about the nineties
a Nirvana song small enough
to fit on the tip of the knife that killed
Ron Goldman and Nicole Brown Simpson
a Pearl Jam song so big
David Koresh could build a compound inside it
for Janet Reno to burn down

Let's talk about
the self-commodification of social media
peeling the starry substance from our skin
until we are merely left with a brand
let's talk about love
how they told us it was like the moon
but it is really like the moon's reflection
just a bit of light caught by a body
easily forgotten in a catastrophic splash
and love an act of remembrance

Let's talk about hamburgers
meat and bread and cheese
hitting you at just the right time
let's talk about the news tonight
an outraged man yelled at an outraged woman
an outraged woman yelled at an outraged man
let's talk about how I don't know anything
except our friendship
this bottle of wine
and your smile that has always made me believe
in unicorns flying through blueberry tornados

WISCONSIN

I remember fields so wide
they could grow Civil War reenactors.
I remember the creek that ran through
our land like an old relationship,
banks of familiar yet perilous
adventures and bridges made from the broken

sticks. I remember the woods
that still haunt my dreams with
shipwreck trunks of elm and ash and oak
pulling the land down into an alien ocean,
the dogwood rising to look
me in the eye with a Shakespearean speech
of red stems. I remember the seasons

that felt closer than the neighbors.
Winter had a drinking problem,
not waking up to melt the snows till noon.
Autumn was a handsome redhead,
too shy to tell the girls his feelings
until it was too late. Spring was middle-aged;
rediscovering herself through yoga,
bending and twisting with new life—
but her joy seemed kind of fake.
Summer was relaxed, always eating peanuts.
Born into wealth, he smoked such long cigars.

I remember myself on this land,
exposed where no one could see me;
not happier, not better,
just trying to find myself lost in the woods.

HOMELAND

A coonskin cap, soft
as the lies in a history textbook,
tail swinging back and forth
over my shoulder. My parents
once talked me into wearing this
mountain man monstrosity,
scavenger fashion perched
on a hat rack in an overpriced gift shop.

This flag for a nation of boys lost
in exploration flies over
the American idyll of cabin
and lake. Here there are
campfires and ghost stories,
flaming marshmallows hissing
opinions about how well they
should be cooked. This is
our homeland we make
constant war upon as we honor
the barbarians who built civilization.

KIDS

We went to the shows where
guitars squealed orbits in
abandoned factories, Viking drummers
summoned Berserkers with a thud,
the pale faces of bassists
flickered like candles in the shadows,
the singer's rage was bottled
in pomposity but sometimes a little

feeling leaked out. For kids this is
the excavation of a revolution,
the old ideas of youth
dug up in tombs of leather and tattoos.

Friendships feel like runes and we
are less interested in deciphering them
than surreptitiously peeking
at their mystery. I was lost until
someone said they loved Nine Inch Nails too
and afterwards it felt so peaceful to rest upon

a new solidity. But we were young
and the heart hurts for the hurt hearts.
When I lost my virginity the girl
didn't tell me she had a boyfriend.
Three friends jumped me in an alley
as all my other friends looked on.

They left me to bleed with the old
ideas of youth. Betrayed, I threw rocks at them
and shouted. Then I slowly let my pain
become the river to carry me through.

JFK

Oh to love my country
enough to ask her,
"what can I do for you?"

But this blood-soaked ground
cannot absorb my affection,
the rivers of the great
Midwest will never carry
grim thoughts. How should one

love a country? A dying soldier
is only human for muttering
the name of his wife
instead of the colors on his flag.

And let's not forget,
we hate each other.
Coastlanders don't trust
the sailing cows of the inland,
inlanders cast their nets
but don't like the corn they capture

on the coasts. For love
you must leave your country
and approach what
you do not know. Approach
an emptiness, yourself empty;
to die in this way, to live
in a nation of "hello."

HEALING

I need healing
your hands and eyes and mouth
I need courageous snow upon my eyelids
I need Rocky Mountain canyons
to come live inside me
listening to Adele and Amy Winehouse
at full volume in the early morning
I need the monarchical octopus on the throne
to shake my shame away

I need healing
your hair and breasts and thighs
I need the vast sunset
to touch her pink toes in the east
before sighing the names of disorders
I need you to know I'm not crazy
even though I showed up just now
with all my clothes in plastic bags
and all my thoughts in a necklace of poison apples

I need healing
your style and fight and mind
I need to listen to you and your mess
the clean loneliness that gets on everything
I need curtains to keep out the darkness
turning windows into punctuation marks
separating all my loves
I need to be able to look you in the eye
as you're looking away from me

WORD

If a picture is a thousand words,
then a word is the scribble that makes a sound
with no audible traces. It is
separate shapes of space
combined into time's duration.
Haunted memories, future loves,
watered-down beer; even misspelled
a word will still surround you.

A kind of mirror, a single word may shatter
into a hundred warring countries.
Words are human, we didn't create
rocks but we thought to call them that,
and every word we speak has a lineage.
We will never become gods
with family trees growing on our tongues.
Did Jesus become a man the moment
he said, "Abba?" But even to say,
"I don't have the words"
is to admit there's a God somewhere.

The poet is here to fit as many
pictures as possible in a word,
after that it never hurts to cram
a dead celebrity in there too.
I've been known to stuff a flag
inside a verb on occasion, and don't forget
a word is a great place
to hide a gun if you're a poet
running from the law. But for now, I offer
these high and low words to you,
letters filled to the brim
with all my lost imaginings.

UNFAMILIAR

Walking the streets
of an unfamiliar town
the adobe slips into my soul
waves of crashing rock

The emptiness has followed me here
it makes every passerby a shadow
with limbs of electric bolts

Loneliness is expected in this desert
I peer into the windows
of the closed art galleries
the paintings in these dim rooms
look like senile kings
still holding sway over ruined courts

I contemplate the old cathedral
the pine cross and the plaster Virgin
the courtyard of stones
crackling underfoot in Satanic mockery

Back on the street the cars race by
alone I feel like a stage performer
for the nameless faceless driving past

Suddenly I whip around
and grab my crotch
shaking my head maniacally
abandoning the solitude of ambition
it's the least I can do

SUBMERGED

Oh water
shawl of the drain
thrown on when the sink
entertains guests of dishes
in the surprises of your sparkly chaos
yards become fun muck
you entertain us all
with your New Age songs
when the faucet is turned on

But the lukewarm water
I've left in hot cars
has glared at me sullenly
like a teenager I've let down
the water of my shower
has tried to convince me she's not there
while I recount my recurring dreams
of three-headed unicorn pirates

When Kevin Costner went to *Waterworld*
he drank his piss as water
when Jesus turned water into wine
how gently he must have combed
her wild hair back
tying it with vines
applying rouge to her cheeks
fastening the grapes on her dress
oh water
would I have recognized you then
was your chaos so gracefully discarded

BURDEN

We can't escape the heat
there's no AC in this city
so even in this dark room
the sun peeks between the blinds
exhibitionist watching me as I sit here sweating
that sick bastard is having fun outside
wearing nothing but a trench coat
rain boots and tighty-whities
exposing everyone he sees

I'm listening to The Beatles
songs overjoyed with sadness
dancing with my elderly inner child
so many are talking about politics today
so many are outraged and upset
and they will be again tomorrow
it's like another layer of this heat
making us feel sticky and grotesque
as we all take more and more clothes off
revealing stretch marks and scars

Maybe I'll move to Svalbard
find a shack so I can hide
from polar bears cruising the streets
like hip teenagers skipping school
it will be cold there
like the love that makes you hold on
this room will have to do for now
the sun is flashing friends of mine
mocking them as they run away
the darkness in here is light
like black flames engulfing depths
and imaginations in prehistoric caves

MOTH

A moth flew at me in the shower
this morning. It came through
a crack in the curtain. Without
my glasses on, it seemed
like a piece of the wall had
sprouted wings and decided to attack.

The moth disappeared after soaring
past my nose and I was terrified.
It could have been anywhere
on my naked body, a blur on a horizon
reaching out a tentacle to strike my leg.
I whipped around back and forth—
frantically splashing water—eventually
willing myself to forget this
fuzzy horror rubbing its parts
across the steam. As I

was drying off, the moth slipped past me
and out the open door into
the bedroom. I hunted the creature;
it dived at my nipples, fighting bravely.
Finally, I slammed it with a magazine,
this menace inside me
blurred just outside my periphery.

SEAGULL

Nothing so beautiful
as a seagull flying between skyscrapers
while I slouch in the traffic
of the early morning commute
the seagull circles like rings
around a distant planet
it glides like ropes
were pulling it from the ground
it looks so tiny
next to civilization's massive metal teeth
and yet I can see it so clearly
like the face of a beloved friend
outline as permanent as the Parthenon
bird soaring brokenness
through disappointed hearts

Cars honk and sirens blare down here
thought-leaders in Audis
cut off janitors in rusty bogs of van
a homeless man walks out
from an encampment
crossing the freeway with his dog
in his silver hat he looks like a shaman
about to release our cars from bondage
instead he yells obscenities
while his dog scratches up the cars
the seagull is gone now
I can still taste the image on my lips
and I want to remain in that
morose Eden of dying trees
that bear such succulent fruit

WADING

As I wade in Lake Washington,
speedboats cause cold waves
to paw at my knees like a dog
asking for more treats. This is
what passes for a beach in Seattle,
a pubescent moustache of sand
under a grassy nose. There
is quite a crowd, women (mostly
mothers) talking in the shade.
My daughter is playing. She and
the other kids are throwing toys
so that they glide upon the water,
bridges of skids the lake

can't pull down. I'm standing alone
a few yards from the shore.
My feet are submerged in black
and orange moans that extend
outwards, connecting my feet
to the docks across the lake
and the hulls of the boats racing.
The lost tell their secrets down there.
In my head, I hear my own answers
to the moaning, pebbles and
gold rings sinking to the bottom
of a thought. But to the people
on the beach I must smile, I must
somehow try to fill them with comfort.

ONCE

I loved you once,
I still love you.
When we met for coffee last month,
you told me about your divorce
and I wanted to say
that you'd be in my prayers
but then the sun would have set
behind your breath only barely hiding
the peaks and valleys of your disappointment.

So I'll just say,
I loved you once,
I still love you.
Your face in the Boise winters
was a snowscape with kind red cheeks
carefully wrapped in a scarf...
But maybe I shouldn't mention that

so I'll just say,
I loved you once,
I still love you.
This is a love without desire;
traces of love left in the snow,
reminding me your lovecat roams.
I miss you tonight, we could be
drinking beers, laughing
at old mistakes, wondering
if we were pranked by the clouds
or if the sky was just never there for us.

Instead, I'm lying in the dark
swatting away the smoke
from Sleep's last cigarette,
thinking about how I still once loved you.

ENDING

The sun falls upon us like the white
veil of a bride
before vows are uttered.
Tonight, the streets are redolent

with a similar ending. I pass
a woman in a hijab,
a smile flower breaks through
her cliff face with such force it
scatters pebbles to the depths below
and shakes my own mountain heart
with floral eruptions volcanic.

Sunlight gleams down on gas pumps,
fast food wrappers, crows,
cigarette butts, and discarded shoes.
And what is it
that's about to end? The breeze,
our love, our country?
A species we will never meet
killed by our civilized invitation?
Maybe some part of myself
whom I'll never meet, molded

from the copper air of my pain
and tossed carelessly
to the sidewalk like a lost coin
as I look for a shelter of love.
Maybe it could have saved me,
maybe it would have enslaved me.

LISBON

Our sex last night was so good
I've retained my hard-on
for most of the day. I'm not
even sure it ever retreated
in the normal folded-umbrella-in-a-puddle-
on-my-leg kind of way.

Maybe this is because
with you on top I felt
your vagina entering me
with the soft ground of a hill
penetrating the windows
of a new development,
gently pouring an architect's vision
into the earth. It was nice
to stop worrying about my dick for a while.

Virility isn't everything—it's not even
for us—and at its most powerful
it's barely a gust of wind
blowing an Iowa clothesline.

If a man can give up the ghost
in sex—let his penis tremble
spasms of joy without seeking
gratification—then he can
burn distractions inside the flame
that delight merely orbits,
see Lisbon as it must appear to
a creature at the bottom of the sea.

ANGELS

I have met angels
despite those times I spent
searching for happiness until my sadness bled
crying my car through traffic
swerving between tears and bumpers

But I have met angels
always dressed modestly
always with a kind word
like the skateboarder who called me a good dad
as I felt ashamed for yelling at my kids
when I looked back he had vanished
this is how the Lord works
you may get the crown while losing your eyes
you may see perfectly for eighty years
without ever attaining your desires
you may look out from upon your throne
and see a crown in the sky raining eyeballs
and feel both dread and brokenness

Like crushed old men and pregnant teenagers
I have heard angels
maybe they weren't angels
maybe for them to be angels
we have to doubt a little
like how a country can only be a country
if there are lines to mark its end
the angels sing praises to God
they spin sirens into oboes
they raise lonely sobs like a curtain
and the room floods with sax
they pluck the strings of the homeless evangelist
they guide all of our humiliating whispers
into the beat of a victorious drum

WORKSHOP

What can I teach a class that remembers
the Kennedy Assassination and the Korean War?
Their faces look to me like stones
seen through a crack of poetry, a little
distorted but a little more real. Their voices burn
like candles, steady flickers of passion
discussing the stanzas we study. I
am neither teacher nor friend, standing up here.

They are all hunters and I am merely
the barking dog leading them to their game.
What a pleasant excursion upon the downs,
finding a Dylan Thomas refrain in the shrubbery.
Like the dog, I am an emissary of wilderness
chewing on bones of imagery, sniffing
the poetry of the roadside. I love
these people. One is lining up the memories

to shoot in his mouth carnival, one confronts
the evil that swayed in the long grasses
of her Iowa prairie, one flees a drunk
and the shrieking alarm of his fingernails,
one battles the fires burning his attachments.
Cultures bicker before the bishops,
turning vendettas into verses. But somehow, we
understand the trench coat grins in each other.

HANGOVER

The day started badly,
with a U2 song and a hangover.

I think the president said
he wanted to lick someone's asshole
or maybe he called the Dalai Lama
an asshole or maybe he said a war hero's
mother looked like something
that came out of his asshole. The comments

prompted Focus on the Family
to release a twenty-page memo
filled with opaque references to the Bible
and a discussion on how much
the president resembles Jesus.

This was all anyone could talk about today.
The rain suddenly stopped
at noon like a relative who abruptly
leaves a conversation to chop carrots
and avoid discussing Grandpa Steve.

I walked in the new sun.
The wind was combing the hair
of puddles with a merciless brush.
Hungover, the muddled seemed clear;

even myself, even the human
motivations that must have somehow
originated from the dietary needs
of the Pleistocene Age.
And maybe this is why
I felt so sad for the country;

Amazon's great wealth concentrated
and then exploding into
the daily rubble that buries us,

folks peering into coal mines looking
for the rights they lost in the twentieth century.

All of us powerless on these sidewalks,
trying to find a little comfort.
The wind picked up on this one, clawing
at my face. I didn't turn my head,
I just let it pin me.

GRAVITY

I love you
but not right now
it's evening
the sun is out
but he's hiding like a family member
tired of watching us fight
you have the look
of a bitter building
powerless to give chase
to a jet flying overhead

The gold of my wedding ring
can't confine the rudeness
I spill on you like hot coffee
its borders can't keep out the betrayals
you are growing
in our kitchen sink
we're space rocks in a gravity dance
of screams and kisses
rotating around each other's worst parts
unrecognizable to each other now
baffled by our former amazement

I know I love you
but that love is a color
I'm blind to
and now you are green
with the purple lips that once kissed me
and now your text messages
are mere hints of the conversations
that once kept us up until sunrise

MESA

When I finally make it home to you
we're going to have so much sex,
I will grab your Alabama-Mississippi ass cheeks
and kiss your Nebraska neck.

But right now, I'm driving this car alone.
Around each turn, rocks glare at me
as if I'm stuck in one of those dreams
in which I must make my way
through a crowd without any clothes.

The river running alongside me is a bored
stay-at-home dad wearing a white negligee
in curiosity as the kids are away at school.

And out here I'm a rolling mesa, an Egypt
of impotent immensity, powerful in my inability

to touch. The land surrounding my exile
has battered its way to the fifteenth round
of a boxing match, now the hills
are red and purple. I am a sad martyr,
alone in a holy war of angles but I love you.
I want your curves to lick, I want
your breasts for post-coitus pillows.

APRIL

The popsicle stick on the sidewalk
was dropped carelessly like advice
to the grieving. Today was unusually warm—
seventy degrees in April. It felt like
an inappropriate gift from a rich oil tycoon,
a diamond ring just to get in my pants.
Maybe someone was so excited about the heat
they ate the popsicle with absolute
abandon, red tongue accosting pedestrians
as if it belonged to a vampire who figured out

a way to defeat the sun. Now the popsicle stick
is swarming with ants, there must be
some sugar soaked into the wood.
Their hard work looks disgusting as if
tenacity is nothing more than a festering sore
and success can only be achieved through
the carelessness of something greater.

I just got a bill, my twenty-year-old car
needs $2500 in repairs. On the news,
all the petty statesmen are being rolled up
with the lint. Nearby, the wind lifts
some flowers in a bush of snowbrush
and it looks like a happy girl in a sweatshirt
lifting her hood. The kind of beauty
no one can achieve but everyone remembers.

POP

Getting all the feels with SZA tonight
as that rack of wine from yesterday
makes its way through my wrists and ankles

Sometimes a voice
can bury its dead in your heart
there is a benediction of birds in a
soaring procession of sounds
and a fallen hero enters whose sword flashed
red chills of spinal shadows
to defeat the dragon highway smile
thus you are grateful to have this esteemed stranger
who is now buried alongside
all of your familiar sins

Henceforth there is something of the hero
in what you've invited into your dirt
something to remember
when a lover discovers those emails
when your own child looks deep into your eyes
and despises you
even if it's just another pop song
especially if it's just another pop song

When I'm sober
I'm going to take my wife's hand
and finally do something noble

MOVING

Today, we're moving out of the neighborhood.
Everyone loves you until they don't,
faces climb mountainous expressions
so they can stay above it all. I haven't felt

at home here since they closed the record store
to open a bank and demolished the sports bar
to build expensive condos. But I will miss
this hill from which I watch the clouds

to better understand all of their enduring
phobias. I will miss the bookstore
and its rows sprinkled with the evidence
of an owner's genius like a crime scene.

I will miss the best tacos in Seattle;
the grateful crunch, the soft rush,
the dirty restaurant that's never been cleaned.
Our living room is a mess of memories;

a church group once confessed their problems
here, my wife and I fought and made love
on this couch, when my daughter crawled
for the first time her little rebel fists punched

this oppressive carpet. But after this evening,
I'll never see this room again. The last
of our voices will fade ... and empty,
the room will slowly regather itself.

CLOSE

My daughter curled up in my arms
like a hallway left intact amongst a pile of ruins,
like a fresh aroma wafting onto
a staid windbreaker of the past.

I play with the curls of her hair,
they wind around like the grand conversations
of impetuous youth and I'm caught
up in an idealistic stampede. What

a blessing it is to be needed, to be
the mountain underneath a star—to feel this tiny
body pressing close, ears hoping to
be heard as they listen to the world.

ACCOMPLISHMENT

At the park, my daughter climbs
to the top of the slide—
her teeth bared tenaciously
with something greater than will.

Her force of a face
pushes its way through, tiny hands
grip pieces of plastic,
boots find footholds as she scales

this pretend peak. On her back
I see lines of transformation,
like national borders imposing
a vision upon a continent.

When she reaches the top
I cheer her down the slide.
She tells herself, "good job"
and I laugh at the self-congratulation.

She climbs a few more times.
Skateboarders scrape words from pavement;
a basketball bounces, bounces,
clangs a giraffe off the rim,

and bounces again; dogs prance by,
pulling slavish owners by the leash.
What lasting mark will
any of us make with our little fists

clenched? There is no violence
like inertia. The sun finds a way
to break through the leaves,
catching me with a single ray.

CONCEPTION

We fought under a yellow sky
we fought under a red sky

Then we had make-up sex
under the shrub of stars
and a glacier was conceived

God began to paint the ice sheets
the paint ran downhill
and all the pinks and blues
gather upon your face in the morning

Now we're waiting
for the helpless hands
that crush mountains
for the gentle eyebrows
that form the estuaries of our hearts

There are so many changes coming
that will leave at dawn
none of this seems real
and yet we share it
this love that splits malls open
this glacier that wears pride down

BELLY

My wife's pregnant belly
announces himself at the dinner table.
He lets us all know
he's a very busy and important man
with a Brooklyn accent,
"I'm creating a new life in here."

The online reviews are incredible,
he's doing extraordinary work.
Sometimes, I listen outside the studio
to the strange noises coming from inside:
a chainsaw, a fire extinguisher,
an old bike horn. The expectation

is thrilling. Still, does he
have to be so arrogant? Walking ahead
of my wife with his nose
up in the air; demanding hamburgers
at four a.m., pickles dipped
in peanut butter for dinner. He exudes

an unmistakable air of accomplishment.
He's graced the cover of every magazine
with that famous essence of futures.
But it is not quiddity
that is forming on those long nights,
it is haecceity. The more

confident he gets, the more he will diminish
as a specific glory
unfolds. He is not a shaper
of forms. He is just a celebrity
sitting in his studio dumbfounded,
watching eyelids becoming new.

NE'ER-DO-WELL

The summer air has
developed a drug problem
this hulking mass of swirling grey carcinogens
fell face first on the beach
the beach was cordoned off
and we were all told to go home
he was in the hospital for weeks
mumbling baseball scores
after his stomach was pumped

And so the rain came
with her weird parties
we were instructed to wear funny hats
while she played ragtime
on an out of tune piano
but no one wants to hear that crap in September
it was nice to see her gone this morning
when the summer air returned
to swing his body on the rooftops

I was driving when I heard the gunshot
it sounded like a lonely Christmas
a few blocks later
I saw blood stains
on the leaves of the trees
the summer air must've staggered through there
leaves falling in his wake
he left debts all over town
and the cold wind stalking

DITCH

Ravaged by a long decade,
the ditch is deep enough
to be filled with the memories
of childhood experiences we don't understand.
Cars are parked
on the edge like abandoned emotions

(white Dodge van sadness,
the squeamishness of a maroon Honda from 2005).

There is a man in one of them
just staring straight ahead,
his face a whisper with the gaze
of a Roman pillar.

The ditch is overgrown with weeds
winding around once-proud poles deposed
by cars and forgotten mischief.
My daughter and I must navigate
this tantrum of nature growing
in the orange dirt. I brush the branches
out of her way. She ducks
her head, intrepid explorer with
a bunny-shaped backpack.

Then we see the lilies. Yellow
and drooping with shyness,
miracles afraid to look us in the eye.
A hope that isn't hopeful
on this street with no sidewalks
where all possibilities lie in a ditch.

SHEDDING

The air is cool (some might say cold)
but it's summer and I'm only ever comfortable
in the long struggle to attain warmth
and yet warmth is not what I strive towards.
I'm in the old neighborhood. It's gentrified now
and the rich folks who ran us out are driving
new cars and listening to rap music loudly,
smiling faces glimmering like skyscraper windows
too far away for me to ever touch such light.

I drove here in a car sputtering misgivings
while I prayed to Jesus. I caught a whiff
of nostalgia or maybe brake fluid as I parked
at the mechanic's. I'm feeling rather hopeless,
my car drives like a heart attack
striking a Shetland pony. I work hard
but only us lazy bastards say that. Still,
I wish the money would stay longer and not leave
at all hours of the day and night like
a wayward teenager getting wasted with friends.

Today, my daughter saw me break down and cry
as I opened the bills. She's only three but
she hugged me and said, "I love you, daddy."
And maybe that's what keeps me here,
waiting for the bus home. I see it now,
coming around the corner. A homeless man
approaches and says, "listen, if you ain't got
much money to help me with I can always
put you on a payment plan." I laugh
as I shed everything to become a passenger.

UPWARD

My son, as I hold you in my arms
I can't stop my mind from considering
the issues of the day. But your
little body pulls me back; that thick

whiff of hair caught by the top
of your head, your eyes carving
the destiny of novelty onto every object.
Nevertheless, I wonder whether
these bloody thoughts will blow

a rancorous breeze through you.
And what kind of a man you'll be—
not all white so I fear not alright.
Is it a grimace or a bullet hurtling
towards you through the dark, empty space
of America? I have waited to write

these lines until you were born, afraid
the pen would bleed you. Now you're here,
screaming sometimes but mostly
attentive to mother's milk; striving
with grabbing hands, face tilted upward.

Your sister is kissing you through
her bedroom wall, she presses her songs
against your forehead. We're here forever
to mess up your plans (a true family).

BILDUNGSROMAN

So tiny this dream
this hope
this cry at four in the morning
this fist clenched and covered in a sock
this mouth frantically searching

But how immense that cry
terror of waking up in a dark pit
where possessed toys leer at you
but how immense those fists
anger at a world one can't control
the clueless family friend
struggling to change this baby's diaper
but how immense the searching
the kind face of a mother bending down
will not tell us why we want to engulf her

So tiny
those seaweed legs
that gathering crowd of hair
never again
to enjoy such immensity

JANUARY

The unlit Christmas tree
is a shadowy house guest
rolling cigarettes in the corner
the blond angel has gone grey
ornaments look like fallen debris
from a hijacked flight

Christmas passed weeks ago
I suppose we're being lazy
by leaving it up
but my daughter
is still wearing a Santa hat
and somewhere in the dark
boughs of the tree
you can still see magic
deeper and more dangerous
winter ice fangs slurping sunlight
and needles poking lies

Two weeks before Christmas
my daughter and I
crawled under the tree
looking up through lights and branches
we saw the last
genuine smile in politics
we saw the tears
of a Dust Bowl farmer in 1936
saving his family
by leaving his land
now the frills are gone
but the tree still holds these memories
it is possible to stretch
your life beyond its time

PERFECTION

I want to be the perfect patient,
resolving disputes between doctors and nurses
by opening myself up so they can stuff
all their metal instruments
into me, creating a robotic rat

to fight Covid-19. I want
to be the perfect father and give in
to these terrorist demands
for CANDY and TOYS and NO SLEEP
so the kids can use our home
as a military compound from which to launch
The Child Insurgency. I want to be
the perfect fan; get the same
haircut, read the same books,
admire the same paintings as my idol

so I can walk into a café
and wipe her fame off the back of my hand.
I want to be the perfect Christian.
Driving the fancy cars
that Jesus would have driven,
I'll hang out with all the billionaires
whom Judas would have wanted to know,

praising with hands raised to mansions
in the sky. I want to be the perfect
American; to see in every reality TV star
the qualities of a great president,
to give all I've got to a shitty job
but to only ever look out for myself.

FACES

Come down to the shore
and share a little social distance with me
I see you glancing up
from your book of Russian history
I've leapt across the oceans
where sock puppets hide their kidnap victims
to get this ring so I don't
want to sleep with you
but I don't want you to go back to quarantine
I will never meet another just like you
even the famous are nothing more
than the memory of an impression
I've read volumes on Charles Manson
yet a postal worker delivering mail in 1957
will forever be unknown to me

Someone has to be intimate with the billions
this broken fence is in the shape of eternity
and I want so badly to touch you
I want months of isolated thoughts
to be inspected by scientific eyes
we can only steal a few glances
before we must flee the virus
maybe I'll never think
about you or the grass you lie on again
but it is a relief when your face fades me

The
TYRANT'S CYCLE

A Pattern of World History Told in Sixteen Parts*

---

* This is a redacted version. Some redactions were made due to an ongoing investigation of the events described, we believe a disclosure of certain details could impede these investigations. Other redactions were made to protect the personal privacy of certain parties mentioned in the original poem. Finally, we made redactions when the disclosure of an investigative technique could impact our ability to gain data in the future. The Imperial Justice Administration is releasing this document internally as both an educational tool and an attempt to gain information about its author. It is not to be shared.

I. THE OLD KINGDOM

In which a nation at peace fails to see the challenges confronting it.

We were happy in our hypocrisy,
buildingtops rose
to mouthingtops praising
the gifted ones who sat
so high inside.

There were things the kingdom
accepted. So many black people

imprisoned. Fatherless
neighborhoods torn apart by crime.

Clandestine immigrants could stay
if tomatoes were picked and bed sheets changed
by that last light of dusk that fades
into a neutral odor. Redacted: Ongoing Investigation

A Christian
nation, so

many cars
and garages
and homeless on the streets.

The drugs came on
like supermodels moving unexpectedly close
at office parties. Music stretched
faces into podiums. Prophets issued
warnings, but who
could listen to so many?

We were so happy when we
were not happy. The coastline
ended our dreams
on a golf course
somewhere in California.

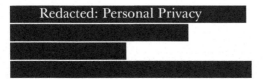

Redacted: Personal Privacy

II. MODERNIZATION/SOCIAL CHANGE

In which the unprepared nation endures a catastrophic event or
undergoes a form of modernization that threatens the established order.

Did you see
a breath blow up the sky,
a skyscraper fall to its knees
for one final prayer? Did you

read the treaty? The government
is exporting our waterfalls
and importing exotic animals
to roam free in the streets.

Did you hear what the king said?
Babbling about *mirrors*
inside his skull—they say
he hasn't left his bed in days.

Did you speak
with the empty bellies sliding
along the sidewalks? That torn
packaging from a youth

that's been devoured. Events
brought us to the future
but when I wake up, I notice
the sky appears from the past.

It shifted here,
pulled by needy clouds
from the time we like
to mythologize. It has stayed

with us as flags fell like veils
over driveways and lawns,
as the events grew so large
they could fit inside each one of us.

Fathers and grandfathers,
with all their eloquence,
could not stop the flaming clouds
from raining ashen

human bodies. Mothers
and grandmothers, for all
their strength, couldn't quite slap
the knives from our hands.

III. WEAK REFORMS

In which a government tries to mitigate these events
or innovations through legislation instead of adaptation.

We're going to have to watch you now.
Watch *Gladiator* fifty times with you,
read *The Secret* and act like it's deep with you.
Redacted: Investigative Technique

Undressing you with our eyes, we
need to ascertain whether you really
have six-pack abs or if that's a bomb
strapped to your chest. Your face

has taken on a different shape
in the sunset, so serene it is
no longer a face but a stream
rushing through a mountain valley.
How can we trust a stream
when it changes every second?
When the drops I see now
will have vanished once I look again?

Like everyone else, we get to choose
the awful things we see. A quarterback
could never commit a crime
but all janitors must be monitored
closely in the nighttime. The fence
only exists to separate low hate
from my hate. Most importantly,
the oil must never cease, it is what we

build your dreams with. Oleaginous hopes
run down pelican necks, funding
terrorist cells from Berlin to Mumbai.
Redacted: Personal Privacy

We said we would protect you. Take heart,
dear friend, our lies are the reason
we must always watch you.

IV. CHAOS/UPHEAVAL

In which a government and its laws are shown to be
increasingly ineffective in solving a multiplying set of problems.

Underwater music;
saxophone sounds
lost in currents,
guitar notes struggle
to reach the surface,
drumbeats drown
in bubbles confining them.

Above, people paddle
rafts down roads
wearing garbage bags.
Rooftops—makeshift stores
where folks buy beef jerky
and a little rest.

Further above,
the king is watching.
Redacted: Ongoing Investigation

Sun glinting off water
promises guillotines
in the swamp.

Hungry and humiliated,
the people are afraid.
The king's defaced statues
shade the homeless
like deformed monks
stretching out torn robes.

A thousand miles away,
soldiers are dying
in a war no one understands,

the soldiers least of all.
They squeeze the earth
inside gun barrels
fired at their own hearts;
then faces get red
and teeth spray out like bullets,
popping and zigzagging
in the dead night.

The king was taught to lead,
never to help. ███████████
███ Redacted: Ongoing Investigation
███████████

He doesn't like the war,
doesn't like this flood.
What is a king?

V. COLLAPSE OF THE OLD KINGDOM

In which a dynasty falls from power, yet still retains some control of a similar dynasty replacing it.

When money is all that
concerns you, what do you do
when you have no more? When the house
they sold you is not your dream
but theirs, some eviction fiction
they must remove a minor character
from, where do you go?
When fame looks deep into your eyes
before smashing your guitar
and telling you she just found you
a job as a janitor, what can

you believe in? Hope, I guess.
Redacted: Ongoing Investigation

The old kingdom is collapsing,
but I've seen a new kind of king
whose Lincoln fingers are pillars
that could support a bold
national monument. He's got that
Kennedy grin, the brothers in his cheeks,
dimples blooming nostalgia.
Redacted: Ongoing Investigation

He wears the crown of the crownless
King who spoke about
the colors of contents and characters.
So many shot dead, maybe
so he could be with us now. Each bullet
forms a bridge from my heart to his.
Redacted: Ongoing Investigation

█████████████████████████

I can't buy any of the things I see on TV
but then there's this man
on the screen who audaciously believes
we're not racist enough to vote against him.

VI. PLURALITY OF MOVEMENTS

In which the fall of the old kingdom leaves a vacuum and creates a myriad of
disparate ideas all vying to become the dominant culture in a divided nation.

Wednesday night at the coffee shop,
the college freshmen try to get to know each other.
It's time to get past
stinky sock soliloquies,
murmurings from monastic caves;
to see the roommate who used all the body wash
as human. Somehow, the conversation
has turned to politics.
Redacted: Ongoing Investigation

It's not going well.

The anarchist Redacted: O.I. says,
"everything created by the state is corrupt
because the state itself is corrupt
like a serial killer turned sculptor
using all his clay for prison shanks."

The liberal Redacted: O.I. says,
"come on, that's ridiculous, we need regulations.
Otherwise, you'd be eating potatoes
swirling in bowls of creamy toxic waste."

The democratic socialist Redacted: O.I. says,
"regulate, that's cute. Potatoes should be free.
The government should build potatoboxes
on every street corner in America
so folks can grab a spud on the way home from a shift."

The conservative Redacted: Personal Privacy says,
"who's gonna pay for all these *potatoboxes*?
The taxpayers. There's not enough money.
Your *potatoboxes* are gonna kill
the elderly, kicked off their social security
so you and your friends can have a snack."

The Tea Partier Redacted: P.P. says,
"don't get me started, we shouldn't even
be helping out those old coots.
Taxes are satanic. God fashioned my rifle
from Wyatt Earp's moustache and the bones of Crazy Horse.
That's all the *help* I need."

The libertarian Redacted: P.P. says,
"keep your god out of this, god doesn't
belong in government. In fact, government
doesn't belong in government. I don't belong
in me, I'm a free freak rocketing through the sky."

The Black Lives Matter activist Redacted: O.I. says,
"wow, I can't believe no one has
brought up race. Systemic violence
has ripped off my head and replaced it with
a basketball, entertainment for white folks."

The LGBT activist Redacted: O.I. says,
"and once again all of you cis people
leave transgender folks out
of these heteronormative attempts
to explain the shifting vagina of the world."

Redacted: Personal Privacy

And so it goes for an hour or so.
Redacted: Ongoing Investigation

Finally, an elderly woman at a table nearby
stands up and walks over to them.
She says,
"what y'all gettin' on about?
Don't you know the president
eats the ghosts of dolphins?"

VII. NEW WEAKENED GOVERNMENT

In which the new dynasty allows greater freedoms for the people and yet fails to unite them or offer them a sense of well-being.

This is everything we've ever wanted.
Why can't it be more? Why can't

the happiness of these days keep its honey
in my throat and heart? Warm amber

blandishments that once gave me peace.
Maybe throats and hearts are not built

for such honey. We need our
quotidian rags of grief and disappointment

that wipe sweet, sticky passion away.
Fanatics do not possess such rags.

Honey drips from gaping mouths
as cultists sing their candlelight hymns.

When the wise appealed to our reason,
didn't they realize how lazy reason was?

Treasures rise and set like suns.
Rays of honey sparkle through the trees

then fade, so last night I stuffed my rage
into the intoxicating pillow that touches

me with bird calls. Distant wonders
slip away and we feel weakened.

Redacted: Investigative Technique

There are so many things requiring my devotion, but I just miss the cigarettes.

VIII. ONE MOVEMENT ACCUMULATES POLITICAL POWER

In which many of the disparate ideas of a divided nation are subsumed by a larger movement.

It began as fantasy; ballads
in the shape of a farmer's sweat,
operas in which wolves rip apart
dragons in the snow, pop songs that saved
the lowliest peasant with celebrity.
The people believed it all

and as they got older
they picked flakes of dead dreams
from their hair. Bitter almost-rockstars
got jobs in music stores, taverns were filled
with military cowards
leading the charge to the bar.

And then somebody saw them.
Redacted: Personal Privacy

We should give him credit for this
at least. He had built entire cities

from the hammer sounds of lies.
But it was the fantastic sounds he wanted,
the kind that rang out
deep in the throat cellar,
vibrating through retinas. The kind
that made everyone who heard them
find a place between the notes.

Replaced on new instruments, it was
the fantasy itself these instruments

tried to play. But those sounds
were gone, lost in the ears
of the deaf and the dead, no one was left
who knew how to make them now.

He could remind the people of how great
the sounds were. He could promise
a world that only he could bring back.
Redacted: Personal Privacy

No one else was talking
about the sounds. They talked
about taxes and freedoms but the fantasy
was the whistling tree husbands
were pulled from, it was the moaning cave
filled with clues. So he strode down upon

the golden escalator; rode his horse
through the beleaguered city,
triumphant from the battles he'd never fought;
walked out on the dais
to address the screaming hordes.
Even when he lifted his voice

it would never rise to the pitch of the fantasy,
but the crowd was so desperate
it had to be enough.

IX. UNDERMINING OTHER MOVEMENTS

*In which the new movement continues to grow, declaring war
on any groups or ideologies not flocking to its banner.*

Tom's hangover felt as if
his consciousness was on hands
and knees slowly squeezing through
a narrow neuron passing pink
synapses in the dark.

He'd been drinking for days,
and when he woke up that morning
he fried some bacon and opened a can of Rainier.

His phone buzzed on the counter
and anxiety fluttered purple leaves
across his hangover. It was a text from Steve.
You coming down today?

To what?
The rally, buddy. This is gonna be incredible.
Rally?
The one I told you about last night.
Oh, I don't know.

*Come on, I'm already down here
waiting in line. I'll save a spot for you.*

Two hours later, they are inside the auditorium.
Signs are being waved, screams
ring out as if it is
the signs screaming, out of control
and dancing in the air; the audience
pulling them down, attempting to calm them.

Tom says, "I don't know, man.
I don't really like this guy. He doesn't seem
like a Christian." Tom had been a deacon

before the affair with his dentist. "Calm down,
it's gonna be great," Steve says.

Moments later the candidate walks out,
"lots of people coming here.
And they're not good people,
I can tell you that. If they were
good people, why would they want
to come here. Not that this
isn't a nice place, but..."

He enunciates waves that pour through
the audience. He pulls the waves back
into himself, makes fun of an opponent,
flapping his arms wildly about. All movements

are absorbed into his movement, as if
his arms are antennas and he is just
the box that can play whatever you want.

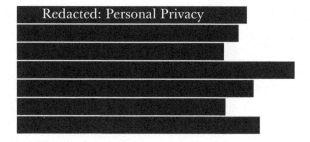

Redacted: Personal Privacy

Tom sits mesmerized, his hangover
has been lost somewhere under the seats
of this auditorium. A ragged scream
crawls up the mountain slope
of his loneliness. Tom can't see anything.

X. REVOLUTION

In which the outcome of a war (violent or non-violent) between
the large upstart movement and the reigning dynasty is decided.

Han spent most of that day in a café
working on a project. The sun was busy
reassuring the urbanites,
like a mayor making the rounds. Everyone

was so happy and good to each other.
Smiles like steel cables
seemed to suspend the city.

Finally, they were going
to win. Things would go back to normal.
Inevitability was frequently
wiped from noses, celebration dripped
from clumsy chins. The first report

from the front came in that afternoon.
Redacted: Ongoing Investigation

It read as expected; a little ground
gained, a little ground lost. Sprinkles
of rain laughter sparkled on the sunny day.

A few hours later, the next report
shattered stained glass window eyes.
Redacted: Ongoing Investigation

A major defeat had pushed the army back.

The sun was setting now,
leaving Certainty to fend for himself
in the city's worst neighborhood. Han
wanted to be with his wife
so he grabbed his satchel and walked home.
His wife was crying on the couch.

"Our navy is gone."
"What?!"
"The ships are burning in the harbor."
Redacted: Ongoing Investigation

They walked to the park at the end of the street
to watch as the ocean tucked the ships in
with an orange blanket before the wreck of sleep.
A family arrived at the park: mom, dad, and kids.
Redacted: Ongoing Investigations

The father spoke, "did you folks
hear about the surprise attack?"
"You mean this?" Han asked.
"No, our retreating army ran right
into another army and was torn apart
from the front and the back.
Survivors scattered,
probably gonna be lost for a long time."
"Shit."
"Yeah, the enemy is only an hour away...
maybe I should stop calling them *the enemy*..."

More people were drifting into the park now
to watch the burning ships. In the dark it looked
like a procession in black robes come
to witness a village beauty being sacrificed.

XI. NEW MOVEMENT ASSUMES POWER

In which a new dynasty, dissimilar to any that came before, takes control of the government.

There were parades without smiles
as if the real parades had died
in the struggle and these
were just their funerals.
The old government
was rushed from power
so quickly the hallways
absorbed the shadows of clerks
and the shadows sometimes
could be seen holding
file folders and running down the halls.
None of the new officials
had experience with anything
other than corruption,
but there were a few generals
who could gather enough
leaves to wage a war.

Reporters hung around
waiting for the new emperor
to speak. His lies raced by,
like the pains of stepping
on unidentifiable objects
barefoot across a dark expanse.
A few were filled with
hope in those days;
many more snuggled
with shock in their beds,
running hands through its hair
and feeding the famished beast.
Imperial power was strange
when the emperor first handled it.
He had never lifted anything
like it, heavy when handled carefully,
lighter when it was demanded.

XII. SINGLE AUTHORITARIAN EMERGES

*In which the new dynasty reveals itself to be authoritarian in nature,
with a government created in the image of one woman or man.*

It started with
a kindness.

Redacted: Personal Privacy was lying down
on the concrete
entrance to the school,

red and black flag waving
above him,
unashamed to show its pain.

The sky seemed so much closer
from the ground,

the view like looking into his
mother's eyes and watching
evaporated thoughts
drift in from New Guinea.

Pushed down,
he didn't want to get back up.

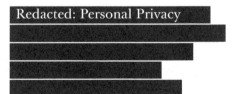

Redacted: Personal Privacy

The ground accepted him,
to his right trees conversed
with dirt and shoes interrupted
stones about to make a point.

After he had lain there
for a long time

another boy stood over him,
face covered in burn scars.

"You okay?"
"Fine."
"Need help getting up?"
"No."

"Okay, well…dude,
you pissed your pants."

"What?! Oh shit!"
"You can borrow
my gym shorts if you need to."

They went to the locker room
Redacted: Personal Privacy

and when they emerged
the bullies were waiting.

"What is wrong with you, kid?
Your dad wipe his ass with your face?"
"Hey Squeabs, is this your new pal?"
"Are you faggots in love or what?"

Redacted: P. P. looked at all of them,
but instead saw
myths burning aluminum faces. He said,

"hey Myers, I guess your mom
didn't pack your lunch today.
What kind of a loser slits her wrists?"

The bully who had pushed him down
began to cry, then punched him.

It was this memory the emperor
contemplated before walking onstage
to shake his fist and address the crowd.

XIII. PURGE OF POLITICAL ENEMIES

In which the authoritarian attempts to stifle dissent.

A.

Goaded by the emperor,
angry crowds attacked
the news, foreheads shouting
and voices turning red. The reporters
so hungry for a story

that was about to eat *them*.
No one was killed, but some
were hurt. A news van exploded
white static pixels from ancient Troy.
Redacted: Ongoing Investigation

Afterwards, everyone waited, not sure
they could forget this.

B.

Senator N. stared at the heroes
on his walls, greatness flattened
into rectangles
that he could hold in his hands.
Or maybe never really greatness,
just a promise written
in a bone structure that someone
framed and sold. He
had made promises too,

had lied to the faces of the dying
then shook them out of his mind
like a match used to light a smoke.

The word *morality*
plunked off his tongue like a cherry seed.

But someone had to address
the emperor. N. had convinced everyone
that his eyes were the blue
of the flag, the blue of patriots
drowned fighting in wars abroad.
So what choice did he have
when they asked him to speak?

Redacted: Ongoing Investigation

The only thing remarkable
about his speech sometime later
was his stumbling walk
to the podium. He talked
about values, words distributed cheaply

and quickly dropped from ears
like flyers to the ground.
After the speech,
the emperor mocked his stumbling;
many of his colleagues went on TV
and asked him to stop
embarrassing himself.

A few weeks later, when everything
was forgotten, he resigned.

XIV. SHIFTING CONTROL OF GOVERNMENT POWERS

In which all political power is seized by the authoritarian and
any independent agency is either subsumed or dismantled.

April had wanted to
visit the capital ever since she was a kid

reading the history books in which
names caught fire,
releasing extravagant plumes of
dates and courage.

Redacted: Ongoing Investigation

Finally, she'd made it
but now there was nothing to see.

The capitol building was mostly abandoned
except for a few vagrants
who slept there in the afternoons. There were
cracks forming on the steps

that looked like the edges
of an old parchment. Many of the windows

were broken, shards oddly cheering
the place with light.
The front lawn was a drunken father
chastised by the sun.

You could still walk
around inside (there was no one

to stop you) but the smell of the vagrants
was rancid and the marble
pillars looked like heads of state bleeding
on newspapers in the corners.

The Supreme Court
was still functioning, but surrounded

by a black fence. Tanks and soldiers
on the perimeter,
dogs with gravestone faces erupting earth
if one got too close.

And then there was
the emperor's mansion, newly renovated

and completely gold. A freakishly tall
statue of the emperor
smirked from the front gate. You could take
a tour if you wanted to,

they might even put
you on TV. But April wanted to visit

the museums that had been shuttered,
see the art and artifacts
sold to the Russians. After a day, she
decided to fly back home.

XV. TOTALITARIANISM

In which the authoritarian's hunger for control now extends to the personal lives of the nation's people, impacting their ability to speak and think freely.

"All rise, the honorable Jackie Pineshaft,
star of such films as
Cuban MILFs 3 and *Jackie's Wet Vacation*,
is presiding. Court is now in session."

"You all may be seated.
Now Mr. Shapiro, it is my duty to inform
you of the rules of TubeCourt. Your testimony
will be streaming to your fellow citizens
across the country. They will vote on
the verdict by either *liking* your testimony
or *disliking* it online. I will then
read the verdict. The camera is
right here, please look into it at all times.
You're off to a good start,
your tie is already getting quite a few *likes*.
Do you have any questions, Mr. Shapiro?"

"Listen, I just wrote a song,
I don't know why I'm here."

"Mr. Shapiro, with all due respect,
you wrote and performed a song
filled with lies and slander
about our glorious emperor. Now
the Supreme Court ruled last year
that First Amendment protections
for freedom of speech only apply
when the form of *speech*
in question is commercially viable.
The government believes that yours isn't.
That is why you are here. I understand
you have brought your guitar with you.
Can you play the song in question for us?"

"Honestly, I just wrote it
when I was drunk, it's not…"

"Mr. Shapiro, if you want to convince
this court of your commercial viability
as an artist, you should probably
summon the courage to play the song."

"Okay. It's called
'The Tyrant Song'."

He wants to rule with an iron fist
but I think it's made of brass
cries so loud when it hurts so little
reverberating off his ass
loves all that pomp and circumstance
but only eats fast food
how could someone surrounded by gold
be so witless, base, and crude
says he's a fighter, he's never fought
could you imagine him in a war
watches TV for twelve hours a day
more makeup than a whore

Cause this is our leader
this is our guy
just shoot me now
when I wake up I cry

This is our leader
this is our guy
just shoot me now
when I wake up I cry

We never elected this foolish emperor
couldn't even win the most votes
some yahoos in the boonies liked him
cause he has a fleet of boats
this guy is such a fucking racist
he's afraid of black paint

The first time he heard NWA
it almost made him faint
he talks about himself so much
the only topic he knows
all the ladies run away from him
as he grabs at their pantyhose

Cause this is our leader
this is our guy
just shoot me now
when I wake up I cry

This is our leader
this is our guy
just shoot me now
when I wake up I cry

"Is that it?"
"Yes."

"Well, it did have a catchy melody...
Let's see what our viewers thought.
Oh no, you received 78,692,329 *likes*
and 91,203,597 *dislikes*.
That means your work
is not commercially viable.
Let's open up our comment section
and see what viewers think
your punishment should be
for criticizing the emperor
without commercial intent.
We're getting a lot of responses here.
I'm just going to scroll down
and select a punishment at random.
Okay, here we go:
remove both his thumbs,
kick him out on the street,
and make him try to play that guitar
with his thumb-less, bleeding hands."

XVI. DEATH

In which a nation cannot withstand the excesses of an authoritarian and finally
gives way to something new and better equipped to face the challenges of its time.

They burned the cities before
they left them; fires pressed upon
the blackness like backstage hands
upon a curtain before it is raised,
a cackling wind stirred the flames
in witches' bowls of ashen muck.

Colorful posters of the emperor
quickly shriveled to black and white
like spectral fundamentalists.
Houses and storefronts burned together;
luxury cushions violence, but bought
by violence luxury must
return to its own violent end.

They walked to the hills, stripping
off their clothes as they went
(each falling shirt or sock an act
of repentance) putting on
the plain cassocks The People had made.
Billboards and mannequins
interrogated their fashion status from afar,

but what did they care now?
The emperor's party had tried
to stop them, had tried to find a leader
to belittle or mock. But The People
had seen deer spring from the mouth of God
and mountains inhaled through His nostrils.

There was no leader in their belief system
and they knew the emperor's party
had no belief system beyond their leader.

An entire nation had been murdered
and they had tried to fill the borders
with a single foolish man.

And so The People walked away
into the night: Christian, Muslim, liberal,
conservative, citizen, immigrant, black,
white, woman, man, cis, trans,
elderly, and infantile. Wearing their cassocks,
greeting a once-conquered land
as a once-conquered people,
all became free at morning's first light.

ACKNOWLEDGEMENTS

I would like to thank the following publications and art spaces where some of these poems first appeared, sometimes in different forms: *The Courtship of Winds, Gallery One, Global Poemic, The Good Men Project, Hex Enduction Quarterly, I-70 Review, Illuminations, Life and Legends, The Metaworker, Metonym, Mobius: The Journal of Social Change, The Nonconformist, El Portal, The Seattle Star, Smoky Blue, Sojourners, Spillway, Thin Air Magazine, Trampoline Poetry,* and *Vita Brevis.*

I would also like to thank some other folks who helped along the way. Monica Jones, Jeff Lareau, Philip Taron, Evy Neff, and Aaron Luoma, I am forever in debt to you for your friendship and inspiration. To everyone in the Bayview Poetry Workshop, I am beyond grateful for all the life and poetry we have shared over the years. To Monique Antonette Lewis, Jason Bates, and all the other writers and editors who have spent time with my work, thank you for believing in these poems. To Mom, Dad, Uncle Pete, and other family members, thank you for the knowledge passed down. To my own kids, Lorca and Elijah, thank you for the knowledge passed back up. And to my wife, as always, not a single one of these poems could have been written without you by my side.

BENJAMIN SCHMITT is the author of four books, most recently *The Saints of Capitalism* and *Soundtrack to a Fleeting Masculinity*. His poems have appeared in *Sojourners, Antioch Review, The Good Men Project, Hobart, Columbia Review, Spillway,* and elsewhere. A co-founder of Pacifica Writers' Workshop, he has also written articles for *The Seattle Times* and *At The Inkwell*. He lives in Seattle with his wife and children.